DIANA

A TRIBUTE

DIANA
PRINCESS OF WALES
A TRIBUTE

TIM GRAHAM

with text by Tom Corby

Welcome Rain

NEW YORK, NEW YORK

CHRONOLOGY

1 July 1961 The Hon. Diana Frances Spencer born, 3rd daughter of Edward John, Viscount Althorp, and Frances (née Roche), at Park House, Sandringham Estate.

1967 Her parents separate.

April 1969 Her parents' divorce becomes final. Shortly afterwards, her mother marries Peter Shand Kydd.

1975 Her grandfather dies and her father inherits the title, becoming the 8th Earl Spencer. The family moves to Althorp, Northamptonshire. Diana Spencer becomes Lady Diana Spencer and begins school at West Heath School, near Sevenoaks, in Kent.

1977 Earl Spencer marries Raine, Countess of Dartmouth. Lady Diana goes to finishing school in Switzerland. She meets the Prince of Wales at a shooting party at Althorp.

1978 Her father suffers a near-fatal cerebral haemorrhage.

September 1979 Starts work at the Young England Kindergarten, in London.

24 February 1981 The engagement of the Prince of Wales and Lady Diana Spencer is announced. Moves into Clarence House, the Queen Mother's London residence.

29 July 1981 The wedding of the Prince and Princess of Wales at St Paul's Cathedral. This is followed by a honeymoon at Broadlands (previously the home of the Prince's godfather, Lord Mountbatten), and then on the Royal Yacht *Britannia* and at Balmoral.

October 1981 The Prince of Wales introduces their new Princess to the Welsh. In her first public speech she addresses them in their own language.

21 June 1982 Her first child, William Arthur Philip Louis, is born, the heir-apparent. He is titled Prince William of Wales.

March 1983 Her first overseas tour as Princess of Wales, to Australia, New Zealand and Canada accompanying Prince Charles.

15 September 1984 Her second child is born. Henry Charles Albert David is entitled Prince Henry of Wales, but known as Prince Harry.

1986 Sarah Ferguson marries Prince Andrew.

1988 Becomes Patron of the youth branch of the British Red Cross. Takes on similar roles in the Red Cross in Canada and Australia.

1990 Visits Nigeria. Soon after meeting people stricken with leprosy, becomes patron of the Leprosy Mission. Becomes Patron of the Hospital for Sick Children at Great Ormond Street. In May visits Hungary with the Prince of Wales, the first Royal Family members to visit a former Warsaw Pact country. In December, during the Gulf War, travels to Germany to visit the families of serving troops.

1991 Becomes patron for National Aids Trust.

1992 Visits Mother Teresa of Calcutta. In March Earl Spencer dies. In June Andrew Morton publishes *Diana: Her True Story*. Tour to South Korea. The rift in the marriage becomes too big to hide. In December their separation is announced by the Prime Minister in the House of Commons.

1993 Resigns from almost 100 charities to concentrate more closely on issues dearest to her heart.

1994 Made Vice President of the British Red Cross. In September given the title 'International Humanitarian of the Year' in the USA.

20 November 1995 Gives an interview to *Panorama*, which is broadcast to 20 million viewers.

15 July 1996 A decree nisi is granted by the courts.

28 August 1996 A decree absolute is granted and the marriage of the Prince and Princess of Wales is over.

January 1997 Travels to Angola to support the Red Cross campaign for a ban on landmines.

March 1997 William is confirmed into the Church of England.

June 1997 79 dresses are auctioned at Christie's New York, raising £3.5 million for cancer and Aids charities.

21 July 1997 Final official engagement, for the children's unit at Northwick Park and St Mark's Hospital in north-west London.

31 August 1997 Dies in Paris in a car crash.

6 September 1997 Funeral service takes place at Westminster Abbey. Diana, Princess of Wales, is then laid to rest at Althorp.

A TRIBUTE

BY TOM CORBY

I F THE BRIGHT SPIRIT of Princess Diana had been hovering behind the windows of Kensington Palace in the week of her tragic death she would have been touched, but also bemused, by the torrents of tributes that carpeted the road outside the palace gate, as well as by the banks of flowers and messages massed against the gilded railings of Buckingham Palace and by the never-ending queue of those wishing to inscribe their messages in the ever-increasing number of books of condolence in St James's Palace. Her practical side would have wanted to scoop up the thousands of bouquets left by battalions of admirers and have them sent to the nearest hospital to cheer up the patients, those people to whom she devoted so much care and attention in the sixteen years following her recruitment to the world's most celebrated royal family. But to the rest of the world it was right they should lie there. The cruel snuffing out of so bright a light leaves a personal and public void that seems impossible to fill.

In January 1997, at Neves Bendinha, an orthopaedic workshop in Luanda, Angola, with thirteen-year-old Sandra Thijika, who has been badly injured by a landmine. The Princess is holding Sandra's makeshift crutch.

7

Certainly the outpouring of public grief must have helped Prince William and Prince Harry, who, in the seclusion of Balmoral, the Queen's retreat in Scotland, were grieving for their adored young mother. They, their father – the Prince of Wales – and all the Royal Family, were said to have been strengthened by and 'enormously grateful' for the support of millions of ordinary people.

For those millions, Diana represented a never-ending succession of roles: a glamorous cover girl, with a model's face and figure, she also had the practicality and compassion of a social worker. She made whoever she was talking to feel that extra bit special, and she combined the gift of communication with a strong commitment to changing prevailing conditions. And above all she was a devoted mother.

This multi-faceted personality made her the undisputed star in the royal firmament. Millions of women fantasized about changing places with her, but those who were favoured with her confidence knew that she sometimes longed for the ordinary humdrum routine of their lives. 'They don't know how lucky

Visiting the Shri Swaminarayan Mandir (a Hindu temple) in north London, in June 1997, where the Princess welcomes the attentions of excited school children, despite concerns of security people.

9

The changing faces of Diana: from 'shy Di' in 1981 to the confident and stylish Princess recognized across the globe.

they are,' she once remarked. She wanted to be the 'Queen of people's hearts', she said in 1995, in her famous BBC *Panorama* interview. It was a rather theatrical expression of a very heartfelt emotion. And in death she has become the 'People's Princess', a title she would have been happy and proud to receive.

Her thirty-six years had many of the elements of classical tragedy: an unhappy marriage, which started off so full of hope, and optimism, to a man who is basically as kind and as caring for the less privileged as she herself, but it all went horribly

wrong, caused by an unforeseeable combination of fateful circumstances.

Yet in her years as the wife of the Prince of Wales, and then later as the mother of the heir-apparent, there is no doubt that Princess Diana popularized the monarchy in a way that none of her predecessors as Princess of Wales could have contemplated. Her wedding was called a 'fairy-tale', but she was no stereotype princess, and in the history of the monarchy there has been no other princess quite like her. But neither had any of her predecessors had to live the way she did. They may have had to cope

with war, plague or dynastic strife, but they did not have to survive permanently in a glaring spotlight. And Diana's two immediate predecessors, Alexandra of Denmark and Mary of Teck, had the advantage of a respectful, even obsequious, press.

Princess Diana was labelled by the media in many ways. Her first incarnation was as a sweet and unassuming kindergarten assistant, the Sloane Ranger who in her innocence posed for a photograph wearing an almost see-through skirt with the sun behind her. Then there was the young bride who became a fairy-tale

princess in a glittering transformation scene in St Paul's Cathedral, emerging on the arm of the man who had been, until that day, the world's most eligible bachelor. But the fairy-tale, despite the wishes of the press, was not Cinderella. Diana was from a family of grandees who had given solid support to Crown and country for centuries.

There was a murmur of expectation in the white-and-gold ballroom of Buckingham Palace at 11 a.m. on 24 February 1981. As the last notes of the National Anthem died away at the start of the day's investiture cere-

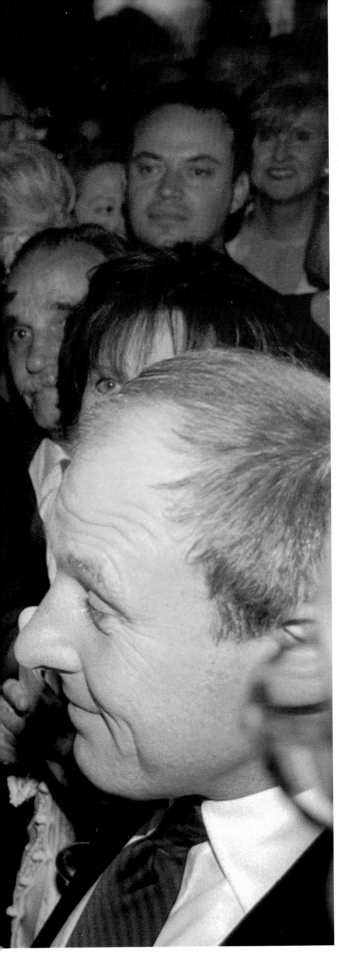

The Princess surrounded by hosts of admirers at the party for the auction of her dresses in New York, June 1997.

mony, the Lord Chamberlain moved centre stage and said that the Queen had commanded him to make a special announcement. Her Majesty smiled with scarcely concealed delight as Lord Maclean read: 'It is with great pleasure that the Queen and the Duke of Edinburgh announce the betrothal of their beloved son, the Prince of Wales, to Lady Diana Spencer, daughter of the Earl Spencer and the Honourable Mrs Shand-Kydd'.

The announcement ended months of speculation, but what few realized was that the nineteen-year-old bride-to-be was completing a page in the illustrious history of the Spencer family, which 251 years earlier had been thwarted in its attempt to marry the first Lady Diana Spencer to Frederick, Prince of Wales, son and heir to King George II. For dynastic reasons Frederick was married off to a German princess chosen to provide a brood of heirs for the Hanoverian royal house. That Diana became the Duchess of Bedford instead, and succumbed to tuberculosis aged only twenty-six. Frederick lived on until 1751, regretting what might have been. He never became King, predeceasing his father by nine years. Thus the engagement of the twentieth-century Lady Diana Spencer and the twentieth-century Prince of Wales was the apogee of more than two hundred years of intimacy and service between the Royal Family and the Spencers, who trace their pedigree back to Saxon times. Their background is as colourful, rich and varied as that of any great family. They also have a habit of turning out remarkable women: some who lived life to the hilt in the fast lane, some beautiful, some political; others simply content to do good. The elegant Lady Georgiana Spencer, married at seventeen to the Duke of Devonshire, was a dazzler, and became a leader of fashion in eighteenth-century society. Her niece was Lady Caroline Lamb, notorious for her ill-starred love affair with Lord Byron, shocking even the libertine society of Regency London by her wild pursuit of the romantic poet. The future Princess of Wales was in exciting company.

Princess Diana's father, the 8th Earl, was, as Viscount Althorp, King George VI's equerry between 1950 and 1952, and equerry to the Queen for two years after her accession in 1952. In 1954 he married the Honourable Frances Ruth Burke Roche, the younger daughter of the 4th Baron Fermoy. The bride was just eighteen, the bridegroom twelve years older (exactly the same age gap as would exist twenty-seven years later between their daughter Diana and her bridegroom).

The Hon. Diana Frances, the couple's third daughter, was born at Park House, a rambling Victorian mansion, in the grounds of the Sandringham Estate, the Royal Family's home. It should have been an idyllic country life, but Diana's secure, happy childhood, with its frequent contacts with the royal children, came to an abrupt end when she was barely seven years old when her parents separated and divorced and she was sent to boarding school. In 1975 her grandfather died and her father inherited the title, becoming 8th Earl Spencer. The family moved to Althorp, in Northamptonshire, another disruption, and one that was almost as disconcerting as becoming 'Lady' Diana Spencer. Earl Spencer remarried two years later, and Diana went off to finishing school in Switzerland. However, she was so homesick that she returned before the year was out, and thus was at

Althorp for a shooting party in the winter of 1977. There she met Prince Charles for the first time since her childhood. Later she went on record as saying she found him 'pretty amazing'. The Prince recalled that she was 'great fun' and 'full of life', but it was a full two years after that brief encounter in a ploughed field before the Prince began to take more than a casual interest in the unaffected, fresh 18-year-old who was such a contrast to the more worldly girls who had flitted in and out of his life over the previous ten years. Now, he confessed, he found her 'really rather stunning'. And as he approached his thirty-second birthday he was not insensitive to the fact that the time was rapidly approaching for him to discard his bachelor mantle.

The early years of their marriage seemed happy enough. Diana rapidly became, in the public mind, a superstar, and at times the Prince appeared no more than an appendage to her glamour. The media's obsession with his wife's appearance frequently obscured the serious message he was attempting to get across, and eventually a programme of separate official engagements evolved for both of them. Diana was transformed, daily, in the newspapers and in people's minds. From 'Shy Di', blushing demurely beneath her heavy fringe, she became 'Disco Di', or 'Dynasty Di'. Then the headline writers created 'Caring Di' and 'Crusading Di', prompted by her tackling of causes where others hesitated, causes that were considered 'difficult', like Aids in the early days after its identification; unfashionable, like leprosy; or simply politically controversial,

A diplomatic choice of outfit for a visit to Japan in May 1986.

15

On her first overseas tour – in Canada – in 1983, the Princess wears the family order of Queen Elizabeth II, a particular honour from HM the Queen.

such as the banning of landmines.

As the constitutional expert Lord Blake put it: 'The real business of our monarchy is not mere glamour. It lies in the professionalism of the Queen as our Head of State, the hard but rewarding charitable slog of the Prince's Trust, the gruelling journeys undertaken by the Princess Royal on behalf of deprived children. This is the core work of the Royal Family. This is where its value lies and where, in seemingly small, undramatic ways, it continues to strengthen the bonds of nationhood.'

Diana instinctively understood this, and she took it to heart as her marriage began to crumble. After the birth of her second son, rumours began to spread that things were going badly wrong. Broadcaster and journalist Jonathan Dimbleby, in his authorized biography of the Prince, published to commemorate the twenty-fifth anniversary of his investiture as the Prince of Wales, examined the marriage in great detail, and described Charles's agony over the failure of his relationship with Diana. By 1986 the marriage was disintegrating 'in the most excruciating circumstances'. The Prince wrote to a friend that its collapse 'has

all the ingredients of a Greek tragedy …I never thought it would end up like this. How could I have got it all so wrong?'

The situation was a difficult one. Apart from the trauma any divorce brings, as mother to the future king, Diana clearly still had an important role to play in both public and private. It was only after much soul-searching, and a letter from the Queen, that Diana finally agreed that divorce was the one possible solution.

There were many repercussions. The day after the granting of the decree nisi it was announced that Diana was no longer to be styled HRH the Princess of Wales, but merely Diana, Princess of Wales. That same day she severed links with almost a hundred charities. In her first move towards a new life as a semi-detached royal, Diana reduced her workload to just six charities in which she was particularly interested: Centrepoint, the charity for the homeless; the National Aids Trust; the Leprosy Mission, with its links to Mother Teresa of Calcutta; the English National Ballet; the Great Ormond Street Hospital for Sick Children; and the Royal Marsden Hospital, specializing in cancer

research and treatment. It was a move which was greeted with understanding by the organizations affected, but with dismay by the general public. It was clear from the timing that the move was made in response to the loss of her royal style of HRH. She was said to have believed passionately that the charities deserved a royal patron. Her loss of status would not be beneficial, she said. It was a positive response to what many had perceived as a snub. But Diana, pragmatic as ever, relied on what her eldest son replied when she asked him if he'd worry that she would no longer have a title: 'I don't really mind what you're called; you're just Mummy,' he told her.

After the divorce she put the previous fifteen years behind her and did her best to create a new life from the ashes of the old. At the suggestion of Prince William, she sold off seventy-nine of her evening dresses in a charity auction at Christie's in New York. Each dress symbolized a phase in her life.

A year ago Diana, at thirty-five, was a much more relaxed, more self-assured woman than the one who earlier tussled with, or was the helpless victim of, her emotions. She could even laugh at her unenviable circumstances. She derived great satisfaction from her landmines crusade for the Red Cross. She was always happiest, and at her best, when

she was promoting some good cause. At a concert given
Her visit to Angola, a country riddled in September 1995
with landmines after the ending of its in Bologna, 'Luciano
long civil war, was a great triumph and Pavarotti and his
focused world attention on the issue, friends for the
attention Diana capitalized on with a children of Bosnia',
trip to Bosnia on the same crusade. where the Princess

And although she no longer served greets her friend.
as patron of hundreds of charities,
there were countless causes to which
she gave her attention and compassion: she made a point of shaking
hands with Aids sufferers when she
opened a special unit at a London
hospital in a determined effort to
explode the myth that simple social
contact can spread the disease. Then
there was her insistence at hugging
young sufferers of leprosy at a hospital outside Jakarta on a visit to
Indonesia, dispelling much of the
superstition which still surrounds
what is regarded by many as a bibli-
cal scourge. She showed keen interest
in the work of Relate, formerly the
National   Marriage   Guidance
Council, sitting in on therapy
sessions, and listening at a discreet
distance while couples discussed their
problems with a counsellor. She
spoke out on funding for the mental-
ly-handicapped, attacked television
soap operas for encouraging people

With her children:
RIGHT: Walking
to church on
Christmas day
1994 with Prince
William;

FAR RIGHT:
Humorous
reassurance for
Prince Harry
during the 1995
VJ Day anniversary
celebration.

to drink (at the same time confessing she was an *EastEnders* fan), and warned how drink and drug addiction could wreck families. On a solo visit to New York she hugged a seven-year-old child dying of Aids and touched the heart of the city. 'No one in this country has done anything so symbolic for us,' said the grateful head of the paediatric unit at Harlem Hospital, which cares for Aids victims in an area infested with drugs, crime and violence.

Diana wanted to meet the most

tragic sufferers – babies born with the Aids virus, the majority of them destined to live barely three years. The Princess believed it was her duty to improve the life of others, and although embarrassed when people put her on a pedestal, was fully aware of her power for good.

Again, showing her growing confidence, in the last weeks of her life her private life, too, seemed to be on the upturn, and she enjoyed a blossoming relationship with Dodi al-Fayed, the forty-two-year-old son of the owner of Harrods, who had for many years been a close friend of her father. The couple holidayed together off the coast of France and Italy, sailing from Nice to Corsica and Sardinia.

Her happiness was evident, and it seemed, too, that finally she had come to terms with her appearance. Blessed with great beauty, she was also cursed with low self-esteem. She, like so many of her contemporaries, suffered greatly to achieve the 'ideal' of beauty paraded through the media. Until these last months, she had always been fully conscious of the impact of her appearance, with-

FOLLOWING PAGES: A warm welcome at the start of a visit to Argentina, in November 1995.

out ever seeming content with it. Although she loathed the 'clothes-horse' image that had become firmly attached to her in her early years as a royal and stubbornly refused to go away, she also loved clothes. And she knew it was partly her glamour which made her such a powerful figurehead for charities and campaigns. As she matured she relied less heavily on the 'armour' of couture clothes, and some of the most enduring photographs taken of her may well be those of her simply dressed in trousers and shirt, walking through a minefield in Angola. For a good cause, when she wanted, Diana loved being photographed, and she developed bantering friendships with some of the regular cameramen who covered her official engagements and overseas tours. She respected their skills and they respected their subject, who they regarded with proprietorial affection. Tim Graham, who took some of the first photographs of the young Lady Diana, was one of her favourites, and received unprecedented access to her public and private life. His work will, as much as anything else, be part of her lasting memorial.

What turns her life would have taken afterwards, no one can ever know, but

Prince Charles with Prince William and Prince Harry by the River Dee, at Balmoral in Scotland, August 1997, before tragedy struck.

it is clear that her commitment to the destitute, the overlooked and the dispossessed would have continued. In order to see her dreams live on, a new Memorial Fund, officially launched on 2 September, just two days after her death, has been created to plan for an enduring memorial to the goodness she embodied.

But in the end Diana, Princess of Wales, is irreplaceable, and unfortunately the myth will no doubt soon replace the woman, perennially young, and bracketed in the public memory with others cut down in comparative youth, like John F. Kennedy, Marilyn Monroe and James Dean. But that would be to do her less than justice. She will be remembered not only for all the good she did, but for the tragic waste of a life cut short, a life so full of potential to enhance the lives of others.

The carpet of flowers at Kensington Palace, the garlands swagging the gilt-tipped railings, the many messages pinned to trees, all spell out a regard beyond her royalty. One note pinned to a bunch of flowers said it all: 'Born a lady, became a princess, died a saint.'

ABOVE LEFT: At the Young England Kindergarten,
September 1980.

ABOVE RIGHT: Lady Diana Spencer and the
Prince of Wales after the announcement of their
engagement, on the steps of Buckingham Palace,
24 February 1981.

RIGHT: 22 May 1981, Lady Diana's first walkabout, in Tetbury, Gloucestershire – the town local
to Highgrove.

The Prince and Princess of Wales walk down the aisle
at St Paul's Cathedral after their wedding, 29 July 1981.

Posing for the cameras at the start of their honeymoon
cruise on the Royal Yacht, Gibraltar, August 1981.

The honeymoon continues at Balmoral, August, 1981.

The Princess in
Melbourne, greeted
by rapturous crowds
(an enthusiastic student
kisses the Princess's
hand) during her first
royal tour, March 1983.

Prince William's first press photocall, in New Zealand with his proud parents. The Princess's wonderful gift with children stood her in good stead from the earliest days of parenthood. Prince William's presence on tour was a break with royal tradition.

LEFT: A happy Prince William is held aloft by his delighted mother in her sitting room at Kensington Palace, February 1983.

With the warm informality for which she was so loved, Princess Diana exchanges the traditional Maori greeting of a nose rub (*hongi*) with a member of the crowd in New Zealand, March 1983.

At a banquet in New Zealand the Princess adjusts her tiara, April 1983.

ABOVE LEFT: On their Canadian tour, the Prince and Princess dress up in Klondike finery for a barbecue in Edmonton.

ABOVE RIGHT: The Princess checks the cameras.

LEFT: The new team on tour.

ABOVE: Princess Diana and Prince William
follow the Queen ashore from the Royal
Yacht at Aberdeen.

ABOVE RIGHT: Prince William came early to
the formality of royalty: a handshake for
Group Captain Jeremy Jones of the
Queen's Flight, Aberdeen airport,
25 March 1985.

The Waleses together as a family on the
Royal Yacht near Venice, Prince Charles
holding Prince William, Princess Diana
with Prince Harry. The boys were brought
to Italy to join their parents at the end of
their visit to Italy in May 1985.

Together at home
in Kensington
Palace, July 1986.

Always at her happiest with her sons, the Princess loved to play with them, and was determined to give them as normal a childhood as possible. Here, piano practice, a puzzle, and Prince William helping Prince Harry as he learns to walk, October 1985.

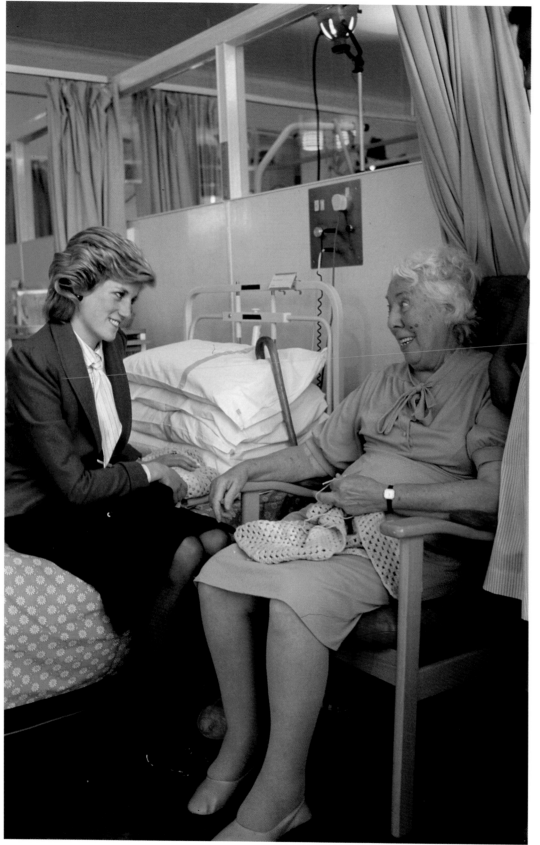

The Princess began
early in her public
life to show excep-
tional care for the
elderly and the sick.
Here she delights a
patient at St Joseph's
Hospice in Hackney,
East London, 1985.

The Princess had a particular capacity to get alongside people from every walk of life.

ABOVE: Visiting her own regiment, she discovers the joys of camouflage make-up with some British soldiers in Germany, 19 October 1985.

BELOW: Young people show her their snaps of her in the East End, 1985.

ABOVE: The Duke of Edinburgh, Prince Edward, the Queen, Princess Anne, Prince Charles holding Prince Harry, with Prince William in front of him, and the Princess after Trooping the Colour, 1985. Prince Harry joins the Royal family for his first public occasion.

LEFT: At a state banquet at the British Embassy in Washington, wearing the Queen Mary tiara – a wedding present from the Queen.

The Princess encourages Prince William to cross the threshold into his nursery school on his first day, September 1985.

Prince Harry takes charge of leading Prince William's pony at home at Highgrove, July 1986.

A wave from Prince William for the rain-soaked crowd watching HM the Queen's 60th birthday carriage procession, 21 April 1986.

FOLLOWING PAGES: The Princess and Prince William together at a polo match at Windsor. As patron of the British Lung Foundation, the Princess chose to wear their sweatshirt, knowing it would be seen by people all around the world, July 1986.

ABOVE: In the Scottish mist – the Princess in the Western Isles of Scotland, July 1986.

LEFT: On the bridge of HM Submarine *Trafalgar*, complete with a borrowed junior officer's cap, August 1986.

FACING: This informal picture in the wildflower border was suggested by photographer Tim Graham during an exclusive session at Highgrove House. It gives a peaceful and intimate view of the family at home, July 1986.

ABOVE: The Princess off-duty – Highgrove, July 1986.

Prince William's first day at Wetherby
School. He is introduced to the head-
mistress, January 1987.

Wearing the Spencer tiara at a
state banquet in Bonn, November
1987. This was the gown that
later attracted the largest bid at
the charity auction of her
evening dresses.

Formal and informal: ABOVE: With HM
Queen Elizabeth the Queen Mother and
Prince William at Trooping the Colour,
June 1987; LEFT: With Prince Harry at
polo, Windsor, May 1987.

FACING PAGE: A stunning
appliquéd gown for a dinner at
the Elysée Palace, Paris, 1988.

LEFT: In Hong Kong, November 1989.

ABOVE: A more reflective moment.

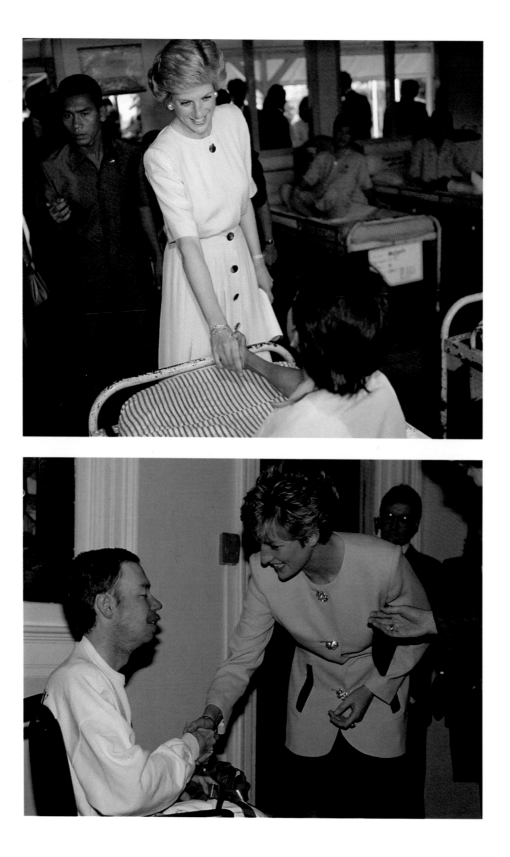

FACING PAGE: Two handshakes that made an overwhelming difference. The Princess insisted on touching both leprosy sufferes and Aids patients, radically changing public perception of these illnesses. ABOVE LEFT: In Indonesia, visiting a leprosy hospital in 1989; BELOW LEFT: At Casey House Aids hospice in Toronto, October 1991.

THIS PAGE, ABOVE: The people reach out on a walkabout in Loughborough, 1990.
RIGHT: Not only the sick but also the elderly were the Princess's special concern, September 1990.

The children's Princess: (from left to right) in
Macedon, Australia, 1985; with the daughter of a
tank commander serving in the Gulf, 1991; at the
Great Ormond Street Children's Hospital, 1993;
on tour in South Korea, 1992; at a school in
Carajas, Brazil, 1991.

Hats galore: ABOVE: With the
Duchess of York at Ascot, 1991;
and LEFT: At Sandringham for
the christening of her niece,
Princess Eugenie.

RIGHT: The Princess developed
her own distinctive style, and
took typical care to encourage
young British designers.

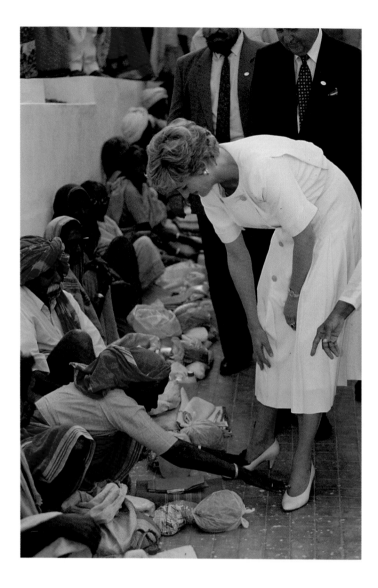

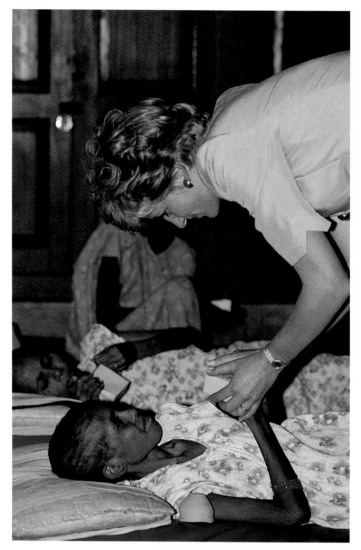

She reached out towards those suffering from poverty and deprivation: in India with members of the untouchable caste, February 1992; and at Mother Teresa's Hospice for the Dying in Calcutta; ABOVE RIGHT: With a HIV-positive baby in 1991 in São Paolo, Brazil and RIGHT: At a family welfare centre in Pakistan in September 1991.

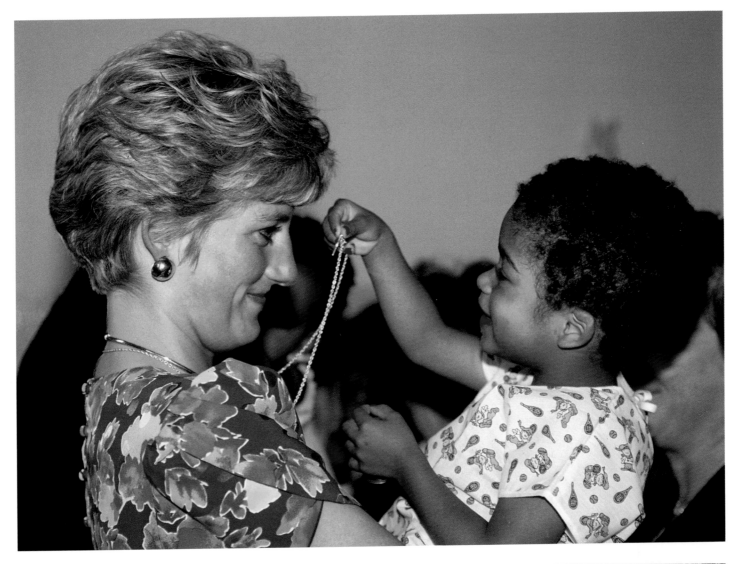

FOLLOWING PAGE: Brazil, April 1991.

The Princess in front
of the Taj Mahal,
February 1992.

LEFT: Head covered
appropriately, admiring
the sights at the Al-Azhar
Mosque, Cairo, and
ABOVE: In Karnak, Egypt,
May 1992.

In Lech, Austria: a last glimpse for the
cameras before setting off after a photocall; with Prince Harry on the way to the
slopes.

ABOVE: A visit from their Colonel-in-Chief for the Light Dragoons in Bergen Hohne, Germany.

RIGHT: With the Prince of Wales at a service in Liverpool commemorating the Battle of the Atlantic, May 1993.

The Prince and Princess of Wales with Prince William and
Prince Harry attend the VJ Day parade. The Princes found
the heat and the vast length of the parade a challenge.

Arriving at Bridgewater House, London, on the
evening the Panorama interview was broadcast,
20 November 1995.

At a lunch given in April 1997 by the British Lung
Foundation to receive a rose named in her honour.

Centrepoint's cold-weather project in King's Cross, London, gets off to a flying start, March 1997.

Arriving at the Savoy Hotel, London, for an awards luncheon, March 1997.

ABOVE: In Washington for a gala dinner to raise funds for the International Red Cross. The choice of a red dress was a carefully considered one, to focus people's minds on the charity in question.

RIGHT: In Chicago for a dinner. The Princess's poise, beauty and highly developed sense of style were never more apparent.

The Princess broke new ground with her decision to auction
her evening gowns to raise money for those causes dear to her.
ABOVE: With Chrisopher Balfour of Christie's, she ensures maxi-
mum coverage for the event by inviting Tim Graham to photograph her with her dresses, yielding the largest possible public
interest and the most funds for the charities.

RIGHT: During the party a humorous moment – a typical giggle
– and her warmth is shared in a different way.

January 1997: in Angola with landmine victims, and walking with body armour and a visor on the minefields, drawing attention to the work of the Halo Trust.

DIANA
PRINCESS OF WALES

1961–1997

ABOVE: The Duke of Edinburgh, Prince William, Earl Spencer (brother of Diana, Princess of Wales), Prince Harry and the Prince of Wales following the coffin to the funeral of Diana, Princess of Wales, 6 September 1997.

PREVIOUS PAGE: Looking at floral tributes outside Kensington Palace, 5 September 1997.

FACING PAGE

TOP: The cortège approaching Westminster Abbey, with the coffin of Diana, Princess of Wales on a gun carriage drawn by the King's Troop, Royal Horse Artillery.

ABOVE: The coffin is carried into the Abbey by members of the 1st Battalion, Welsh Guards.

FAR RIGHT, ABOVE: The Hon. Mrs Frances Shand-Kydd, mother of Diana, Princess of Wales, and BELOW: Lady Sarah McCorquodale, sister of Diana.

LEFT: The coffin leaving the Abbey, surmouted by wreaths from Prince William and Prince Harry, and from Earl Spencer. A handwritten card is just visible.

ABOVE: HM the Queen and HM the Queen Mother watch the departure of the cortège.

BELOW: The Prince of Wales with his sons after the funeral.

A loving touch for the young princes
from their uncle, Earl Spencer, as they
enter Westminster Abbey.

This is a Welcome Rain Book, distributed in the United States by
Benford Books, 234 Nassau Street, Princeton, New Jersey, 08542

Photographs copyright © Tim Graham, 1997
Text copyright © Tom Corby, 1997
Copyright © Weidenfeld & Nicolson, 1997

ISBN: 1-56649-599-7

First Printing
10 9 8 7 6 5 4 3 2 1

Production by Blaze I.P.I.
Manufactured in the United States of America
by Horowitz / Rae Book Mfrs.

Photographs
Endpapers Flowers outside Kensington
Palace.
Front: the day after Diana's death and, back,
the day before her funeral.
Frontispiece At Christie's auction house,
London, 2 June 1997

Title page In Hong Kong

Page 4 In Lech, Austria, taking
the princes for a sleigh ride.

Page 5 Launching a campaign for
Centrepoint, 2 December 1996